STICK

OUT

YOUR

TONGUE!

To my daughter, Katie, a continuing source of
inspiration and forever the center of my life.

—J. B.

To my wife, Jane, and my son, Liam,
for their love and support.

—J. T. W.

Published by
PEACHTREE PUBLISHERS, LTD.
1700 Chattahoochee Avenue
Atlanta, Georgia 30318-2112

www.peachtree-online.com

Text © 2001 Joan Bonsignore
Jacket and interior illustrations © 2001 John T. Ward

Book design by Loraine M. Balcsik

Manufactured in Singapore

10 9 8 7 6 5 4 3 2 1
First Edition

ISBN 1-56145-230-0

Library of Congress Cataloging-in-Publication Data

Bonsignore, Joan.
   Stick out your tongue: fantastic facts, features, and functions of
animal and human tongues/written by Joan Bonsignore; illustrated by
John Ward. --1st ed.
        p. cm.
Summary: An introduction to the subject of animal and human tongues,
providing facts about the unusual features and functions of tongues.
   ISBN 1-56145-230-0 (alk. paper)
   1.   Tongue--Juvenile literature. [1. Tongue.] I. Ward, John, 1963-
ill.   II.   Title.
QL946   .B66 2001
612. 8 ' 7--dc21
                                    2001002931

STICK OUT YOUR TONGUE!

Fantastic Facts, Features, and Functions

of Animal and Human Tongues

Joan Bonsignore

Illustrated by
John T. Ward

PEACHTREE
ATLANTA

Tongues aren't just for licking ice cream cones.

Tongues are for tasting, but that's not all they do. Animals use their tongues in all sorts of amazing ways. Some tongues catch insects, suck the nectar from flowers, or clean fur. Some tongues can reach way under the ground or up to the tops of trees.

Tongues can even be used for touching and smelling.

The size and shape of a tongue can help an animal survive.

Moths and butterflies use their tongues like straws to suck the sweet nectar from flowers.

The tongue of an insect like a moth or a butterfly is quite different from the tongues of other animals. These insects have a proboscis, a mouthpart that extends out and forms a long, thin tube much like a tiny straw. The moth or the butterfly sticks the proboscis deep into the heart of a flower blossom and sucks out the sweet nectar. One moth in Madagascar has a proboscis that is nine inches long. That's about as long as your mom's foot!

Can you roll your tongue into a tube? If your tongue was a little longer, you could slurp up a milkshake without a straw.

The ambush bug also sucks juice with its proboscis, but it doesn't suck nectar.

This little bug, which is only as big as the tip of your middle finger, hides in the blossoms of a goldenrod flower and waits patiently for a fat fly or wasp to land nearby.

The ambush bug seizes the unsuspecting prey with its clawed front legs and quickly uses its proboscis to sting its victim. The sting paralyzes the prey, and the ambush bug sucks all the liquid out of its body. After all the juice is removed, the ambush bug uses its front legs to toss the dead bug's body away.

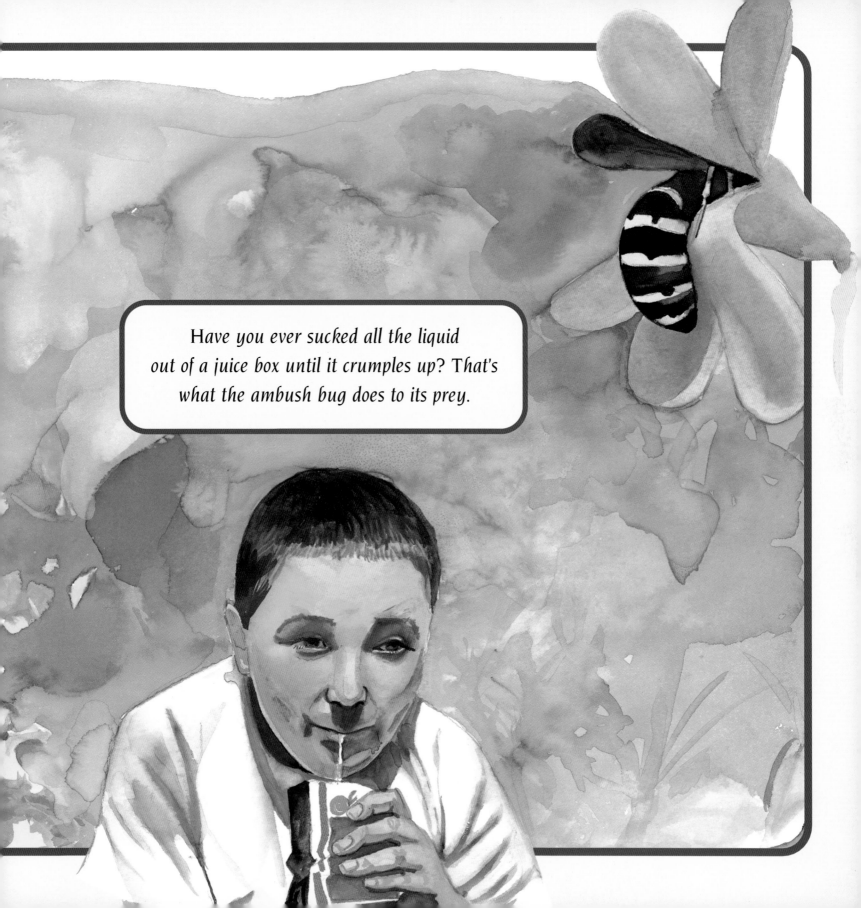

Have you ever sucked all the liquid out of a juice box until it crumples up? That's what the ambush bug does to its prey.

Bats can dip their long, slender tongues into flowers to reach the sugary juice inside.

The long-nosed bat is a flying mammal that lives in the tropical regions of southern Mexico. It pushes its tongue way down into the blossoms of the night-blooming cactus, and the tasty nectar clings to the tip of the bat's tongue.

woodpecker's barbed tongue helps it catch beetles to eat.

First the woodpecker uses its powerful beak to pound holes through the bark on trees, so it can get at wood beetles. After making the hole, the woodpecker sticks in its long, sharp tongue and spears the beetles.

The woodpecker's tongue is too long to fit in its mouth, and that makes storage a problem. When the woodpecker pulls its tongue back into its mouth, the long tongue goes under its jaw, wraps around the back and top of its head, and anchors itself in the right nostril at the top of its beak.

Aren't you glad you don't need such a complicated system for keeping your tongue in your mouth?

T he archerfish uses its tongue like a squirt gun to shoot down its prey.

This Asian fish waits just below the surface of the water. When a bug or flying insect comes near, the archerfish is ready with a big surprise! It sucks in its gills and rolls its tongue against the roof of its mouth, forming a tube. The archerfish uses this tube like a powerful squirt gun. It takes aim and fires a spray of water at the unsuspecting bug. When the bug falls in the water, the fish quickly gobbles it up.

If you should decide on catching a flying bug for your dinner, try shooting it down with your tongue!

Some animals use their tongues to catch fish.

The purple gallinule, a beautiful water bird, and the very unattractive alligator snapping turtle don't seem to have much in common. But they both have a taste for fish and a tongue for fooling. They wiggle their tongues in the water to trick fish into thinking they see a tasty worm. As soon as the fish comes near, the hungry bird or turtle snaps it up for dinner.

The chameleon's sticky tongue
is good for catching flies.

Chameleons are tree-dwelling lizards that feed mostly
on insects but sometimes on small birds and reptiles.

While the smallest chameleon can be held in your hand, the largest grows up to two feet in length. The tongue of a chameleon is almost as long as its body. When a chameleon sees a tasty fly, it flashes out its sticky tongue at lightning speed. The fly sticks to the gooey bulb end of the chameleon's tongue, and the chameleon quickly pulls the snack into its mouth.

The next time you go on a picnic, take along a chameleon instead of a flyswatter!

The long, sticky tongue of the anteater can reach down into the ground to find ants and termites.

The great anteater uses its sharp front claws to open ant or termite mounds and then inserts its long, sticky tongue. The ants and termites stick to the tongue, and the anteater laps them up. What a yummy meal for a hungry anteater!

If you measured how tall a two-year-old child is, then you would know how long you could stretch the great anteater's tongue.

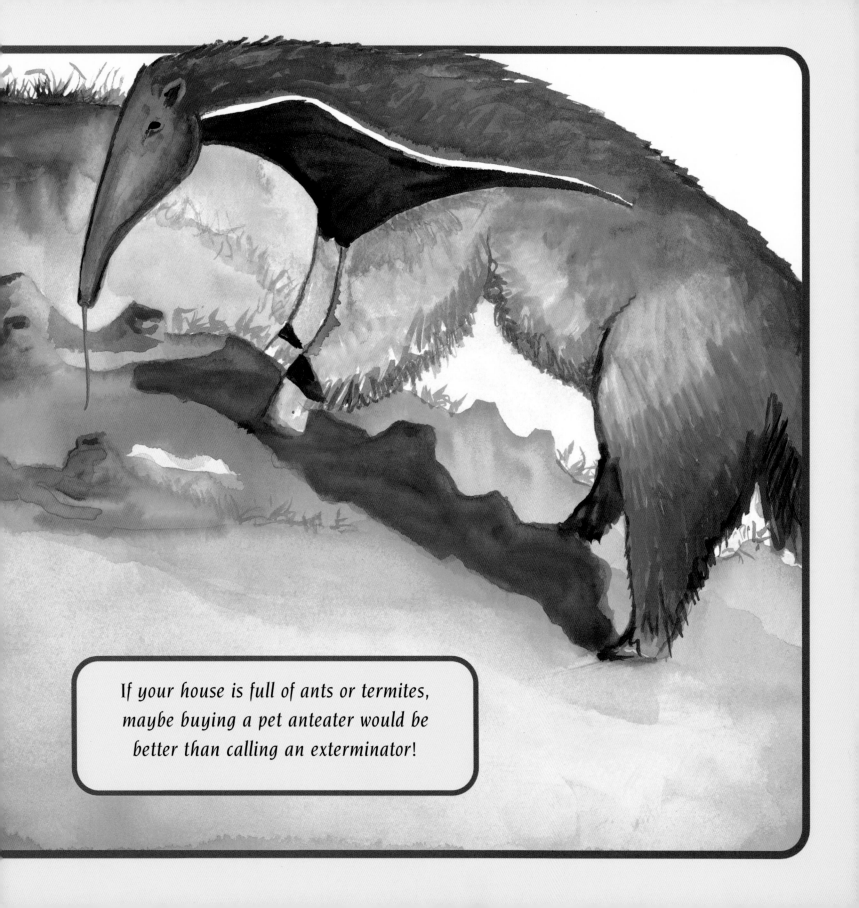

If your house is full of ants or termites, maybe buying a pet anteater would be better than calling an exterminator!

The Jersey cow grasps a tasty clump of grass with its floppy pink and black-spotted tongue.

Because cows have no upper front teeth to bite off the grass, they have to wrap their tongues around the grass and pull it into their mouths. After their tongues rip off a mouthful of grass, the cows chew it with their back teeth.

The long-necked giraffe's head is high off the ground.

This animal can stretch out its long black tongue, wrap it around a bunch of leaves, and pull them from the tree for easy munching.

Can you pick up a pea with your tongue? Make sure your mom isn't looking.

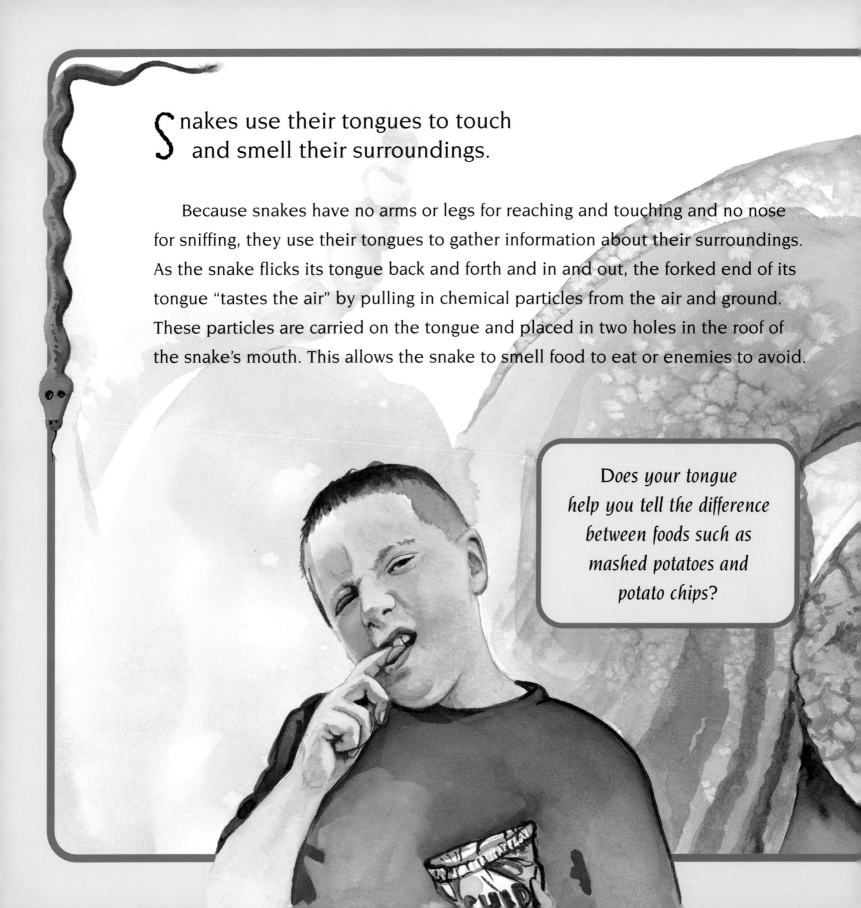

S nakes use their tongues to touch and smell their surroundings.

Because snakes have no arms or legs for reaching and touching and no nose for sniffing, they use their tongues to gather information about their surroundings. As the snake flicks its tongue back and forth and in and out, the forked end of its tongue "tastes the air" by pulling in chemical particles from the air and ground. These particles are carried on the tongue and placed in two holes in the roof of the snake's mouth. This allows the snake to smell food to eat or enemies to avoid.

Does your tongue help you tell the difference between foods such as mashed potatoes and potato chips?

Once they have found food, snakes may use their sense of touch to help them eat their meals. Some snakes use their tongues to feel that the fur of their prey is facing the right direction to make swallowing easier.

Some geckos use their tongues like windshield wipers.

The gecko uses its tongue for cleaning. Because most geckos do not have movable eyelids, they cannot blink to clear their eyes. The gecko sweeps its tongue across its eyes to clean them off.

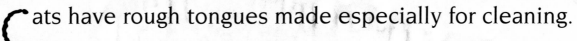

Cats have rough tongues made especially for cleaning.

All kinds of cats—house cats, wildcats, tigers, lions—use their tongues for cleaning their fur. They spend a lot of time licking their fur and grooming themselves. Their rough, sandpapery tongues can clean other things too. Lions use their tongues to lick the last bits of meat off the bones of animals they have killed.

Have you ever used your tongue to clean cake icing off your fingers?

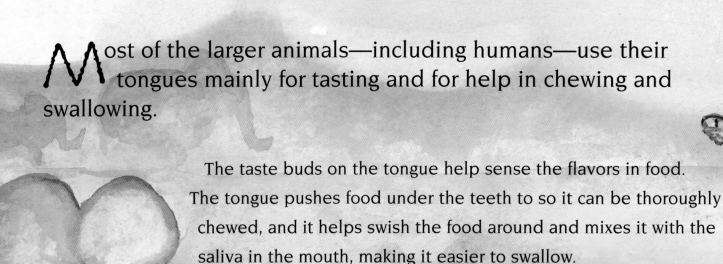

ost of the larger animals—including humans—use their tongues mainly for tasting and for help in chewing and swallowing.

The taste buds on the tongue help sense the flavors in food. The tongue pushes food under the teeth to so it can be thoroughly chewed, and it helps swish the food around and mixes it with the saliva in the mouth, making it easier to swallow.

Humans can do one thing with their tongues that none of the other animals can do. Humans can speak. The human tongue helps form many sounds necessary for speech.

So you see, tongues are very important.

If you hold your tongue between your fingers and try to speak, you'll notice that the sounds don't come out right.

The next time someone sticks his tongue out at you, remember that he is showing you a very special part of himself.

Go ahead and stick yours out, too!